DECISION
ECONOMICS

Some Guidelines for Leaders

DECISION ECONOMICS

Some Guidelines for Leaders

ALFRED R. OXENFELDT

CRISP PUBLICATIONS

Editor-in-Chief: *William F. Christopher*

Managing Editor: *Kathleen Barcos*

Editor: *Janis Paris*

Cover Design: *Kathleen Barcos*

Cover Production: *Russell Leong Design*

Book Design & Production: *London Road Design*

Printer: *Bawden Printing*

Library of Congress Card Catalog Number 97-65794

ISBN 1-56052-434-0

PREFACE

This book presents economic concepts and procedures designed to help executives do their jobs. It is highly selective, discussing only ideas that are directly applicable to business decision and action. Some of these ideas are counter-intuitive; most are not widely accepted and are not easy to understand. To make the ideas that are discussed here useable, it has been necessary to combine them with some managerial, social, psychological, accounting and quantitative concepts and procedures. However, the main thrust of the materials presented are drawn from the field of Managerial Economics, a field pioneered by my former colleague Joel Dean.[1]

Managerial economics contains a body of carefully reasoned concepts related to business about which intuition and common sense often lead to illogical results. The concepts of managerial economics rest upon a factual base of research and have broad application and relevance. They illuminate factual situations and suggest procedures to resolve difficult problems.

The material selected for discussion aims to produce better and faster business decisions. This material does not simply try to improve executives' understanding, it should enable executives to achieve their goals more often and more consistently. It does that by suggesting procedures and concepts that both give insight into complex factual situations and indicate reasonable and logical courses of action.

---

[1] Dean, Joel. *Managerial Economics*, New York, N.Y.: Prentice Hall, 1951.

CONTENTS

I.

BUSINESS OBJECTIVES

I F AN ORGANIZATION IS to be efficient, all its members must pursue common goals. Executives who operate at cross-purposes cancel out one another's efforts. To insure that executives pursue the same goals, top management should prepare a clear and detailed statement of its objectives. Executives who know their organization's aims will know how best to direct their efforts.

Many firms have statements of "corporate philosophy," "credos," "mission statements" and "vision statements." These help to direct the activities of the organization but often are so general that they are compatible with many different strategies and programs. Focus is needed to provide direction and coordination at all levels of an organization. A common focus can best be achieved by constructing a hierarchy of objectives.

Since all organizations have many objectives, it is necessary to organize them to clarify their relationships. Invariably, some objectives conflict—many are means for achieving other goals. Also some are short run and may conflict with other long-run goals. To deal with the enormous complexities that result, the head of an organization should sort out the objectives and communicate them in a way that is clear and unambiguous to everyone.

A useful structure is a hierarchy which separates goals by "level": (1) The "ultimate goals," which are the few key goals that measure the success of the organization, and (2) the "instrumental goals" needed to attain the ultimate goals. The hierarchy also highlights conflicting goals and indicates alternative methods of achieving each ultimate objective.

It is not easy to develop a sophisticated hierarchy of objectives. However, the usefulness of such a hierarchy in formulating business strategies makes it so valuable a managerial tool that it is worth the effort.

Objectives Defined

Before explaining how to create a hierarchy of objectives, objectives must first be defined. Basically, objectives represent unfilled wants—things an organization wants but does not have. As indicated, objectives vary by level. Some wants are ultimate—they are wanted for their own sake. Most of a firm's objectives are instrumental. These goals are pursued because they help to gain higher-level objectives. To illustrate: Top management may be especially anxious to increase the price of its common stock in the near term. It wants to do so in order to make an acquisition on favorable terms. It wants to acquire that firm to increase its market power in its industry, which would increase its profitability. As a result, management would consider the firm to be more successful. In that illustration, all but the goal of achieving business success are instrumental goals.

Common Errors in Formulating Objectives

Not uncommonly, top managements treat instrumental goals as ultimate goals. If so, those goals will be pursued far beyond the point where they help to achieve a higher-level goal. For example, a firm's cost to raise the price of its common stock may greatly exceed its contribution to the firm's profitability and the company's success. Many firms get locked into the goal of increased market share, and they try to increase market share even when this goal reduces profits and stock prices, which are higher-level goals.

Some businessmen make frequent use of "priorities." That is, they label certain goals the most important. As a result, other less urgent needs are intentionally neglected so that the firm's chief priority can be achieved. That can mean that important needs involving small expenditures are neglected in order to make a trivial increase in the chief priority.

Rather than set priorities, management must allocate its efforts and resources among competing uses in a way that produces maximum benefit. Those uses that contribute most to the firm's ultimate goals would get the largest share of the firm's resources; other claimants would get some resources, because small amounts can yield considerable benefit and prevent serious damage. The "equimarginal principle," presented later in this chapter, explains the reasoning process by which top management most rationally allocates its resources among competing demands. Rational resource allocation produces far higher returns than priorities.

Many executives apparently believe that they have dealt with the problem of objectives by preparing statements of philosophy, mission, credo, and so on, combined with a strong emphasis on maximizing profits. Even this combination of guides does not give members of the business as much direction as they require. Philosophy, vision and credo statements often confuse members of the organization because of apparent conflicts with the goal of maximizing profits. Many members of organizations regard such statements as window dressing and irrelevant to their actions and decisions. In any event, credo statements plus demands for maximum profits do not address the common conflict between short-run and long-run profits.

I do not suggest that vision, mission and philosophy statements are useless or irrelevant—though some are. These statements become a real and vital force in company operations when supported by a carefully developed structure of specific objectives. The most useful method of organizing a firm's objectives is by stating them in hierarchical form employing a *means-end logic*.

How to Construct a Hierarchy of Objectives

It will help to understand how to construct a hierarchy by using a very simple illustration. The *end product* is a structure that indicates the firm's ultimate objectives and the different means by which the firm might pursue them. Recall that a hierarchy indicates the different levels of

BUSINESS SUCCESS

Survival	High short-term profits	High long-term profits	Good community relations

Figure 1. Hypothetical ultimate goals for a firm

instrumental objectives the firm must attain in order to gain the firm's ultimate objectives. It also can and should indicate the relative importance to top management of the firm's ultimate objectives.

Figure 1 describes a hypothetical firm that has the following ultimate objectives: survival, high short-term profits, high long-term profits and a good reputation in the community. (Top management defines business success as consisting of these four goals—and business success is the ultimate goal.)

Conflicting Ultimate Objectives

These four goals clearly could conflict. Increases in short-run profits often come at the expense of lower long-run profits as when management delays repair and maintenance, postpones training and reduces advertising to increase current profits. The converse: A firm may accept a decline in current profits in order to increase future profits substantially. In addition, the goal of survival militates against taking risks which could mean turning down attractive investments at the expense of both short- and long-run profits. And, to maintain the goodwill of the community often requires a firm to forego actions that would raise both short- and long-run profits.

In constructing the hierarchy, we would list the most attractive feasible measures of attaining the firm's four ultimate objectives. Specifically, by what means would the firm seek to maximize short-run profits? Again the first step would be to identify the following instrumental objectives: increase sales, reduce costs, add distributors, enter new geographic markets, etc. These instrumental objectives also conflict because measures to reduce costs often reduce sales and compete for limited financial resources.

To carry the process one step further, let us examine the instrumental goals for achieving higher revenues. The firm might increase its advertising expenditures, add salesforce, provide added training for its present sales team, improve customer service, etc. Again, these measures represent conflicting demands on the firm's limited resources. Large expenditures for any, let alone all, of these activities could threaten the firm's very survival. Thus, firms face not only conflicting objectives but conflicting demands for resources.

This simple illustration indicates that considerable time and careful thought are required to prepare a sophisticated hierarchy of objectives. In the process, top management will make its most crucial decisions and do so in full awareness of all of the ramifications of their decisions. Moreover, a well-constructed hierarchy prepared by top management will represent a valuable document for informing other levels of management. More important, the very process of constructing the hierarchy will provide top management with an enriching and enlightening experience that should tighten the bond uniting the firm's management team.

Where to Start

A hierarchy of objectives can be prepared "top-down"–
that is by starting with the firm's ultimate objectives and
descending the hierarchy level by level. One would list the
most attractive means for achieving each of the goals. It is
also possible to start at the middle of the hierarchy by list-
ing the firm's current major activities and asking, "what do
we gain by doing this?" The answers should direct us to
higher-level objectives. We could also descend the hierarchy and ask what is required to achieve the starting objectives. It is wise to employ both the top-down and the
"middle-up-and-down" methods.

To illustrate the middle-up-and-down method, one
can use as the starting point such things as the goal of increasing sales. Management would indicate why it wanted
higher sales, thus going up one level on the hierarchy. To
descend the hierarchy, management would consider many

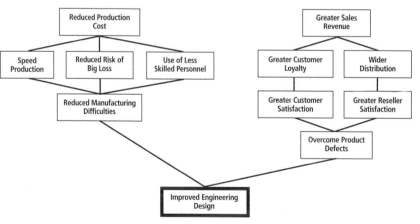

Figure 2.   Higher-level goals for improving engineering design

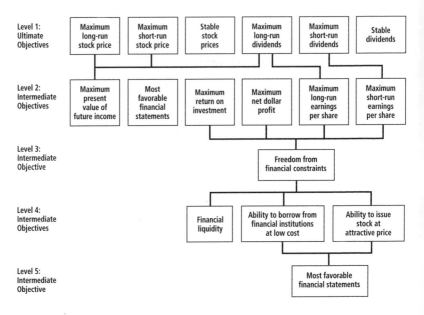

Figure 3. A possible hierarchy of financial objectives

potential means—and list the feasible and attractive ones—
to achieve that end. Before employing these means of
increasing sales (instrumental goals) each must be evaluated for feasibility and effectiveness.

Figure 2 indicates how management can flesh out the
higher levels of a hierarchy by starting with its efforts to
improve engineering design.

Figure 3 present fragments of a fairly detailed hierarchy of financial objectives for a hypothetical firm. Observe
that for each goal at one level, the hierarchy indicates the
most attractive means that management thinks would
enable it to achieve that goal. Each instrumental goal

would help to gain the higher level goal to which it is attached in the hierarchy. The logic underlying the construction of a hierarchy of objectives is fairly clear but much thought and reflection is required if the result is to achieve most of its potential benefits.

Selection of Objectives

If one constructs a hierarchy from the top-down, one starts with top management's ultimate objectives. These are value judgments. For an organization, top management should state what things it wants for their own sake—and not because they contribute to something else. Ordinarily top management would be well advised to state ultimate objectives in broad general terms that invite concrete definition. One way to do this is to use amorphous terms like these: achieve success, gain enduring prosperity, be regarded as an outstanding business, and so on.

The next step represents an answer to the question; for instance, what must the firm do in order to be considered a success? Figure 1 suggests that success in business means survival, high short-term and long-term profitability and community support. These are not the only or best definitions of business success but they are illustrative.

The next step in building a hierarchy of objectives is to indicate the different means of achieving each of the goals listed on the level just described. How, for example, might management pursue the goal of survival? It might mean an avoidance of risky ventures that are attractive gambles, but which could destroy the firm. On the other hand, the goal of high profits might call for management to accept some risky actions but avoid any that would endanger the survival of the firm.

Dealing with Conflicting Objectives

Objectives can conflict for two main reasons. First, they compete for the same limited resources. If the firm devotes large outlays to advertising, it cannot spend all it wishes on personal sales or the development of improved product features. Second, some goals are intrinsically opposed: To get more of one necessarily means less of one or more other goals. For example, to increase unit sales may require a reduction in price; or gaining market power may require large expenditures that would weaken security and survival. Figure 4 indicates how management might deal concretely with conflicting objectives. It indicates (by the numbers in parentheses) a hypothetical management's valuation of different ultimate objectives and its assessment of the effectiveness of different instrumental objectives.

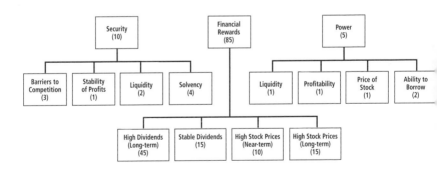

Figure 4. Assigning weights to objectives that could conflict

How can one reconcile such conflicting goals? First, top management must recognize the conflict and deal with it explicitly. For example, management should decide whether to strive for maximum unit sales or accept a lower level of sales to command a higher price. Most CEO's can state what percentage of unit sales they would give up to prevent a drop in price of a particular size.

When executives select among alternative actions, they are making decisions about objectives. Should we accept Order A which gives large unit sales but small unit profit margins—or, should we accept Order B which offers less total profit but uses less of the firm's capacity and permits us to take more additional business? The answer given implies the executive's view of how best to achieve profit objectives.

On the other hand, consider the problem faced by an executive who is working his or her way down the hierarchy from the goal of high income. He or she has identified three ways of pursuing high income. One could criticize the conclusions reached because of failure to identify all attractive alternatives for increasing income or for failure to select the alternatives that would add most to the firm's income.

The error of stating objectives as priorities, discussed earlier, also can arise in selecting among alternative goals. A firm whose ultimate goals include high profits and high community support may decide that high income is the highest priority. Faced with a choice between two large orders, one yielding incremental profits of $800,000 and the other incremental profits of $725,000, the first requiring the addition of 30 workers while the other resulting in a discharge of 25 workers, priority thinking dictates that the first one be chosen. A more reasonable choice would be the second under many circumstances.

Let us consider conflicts that arise when several attractive alternatives, that would achieve the same objective, compete for limited resources. A firm that seeks increased sales can do so by various means: adding items to its product line, entering new geographic markets, product improvements, better service, improved design, increased advertising, more salespeople, better trained salesforce, better customer service, easier credit terms and many others. How should it allocate its sales budget among these alternatives?

The answer depends upon what additional sales the firm would realize from expenditures on each alternative. For simplicity and clarity, our example assumes three alternatives: increased salesforce, increased advertising and improved customer service. To start, it is necessary to estimate what sales increase would result from added expenditures for each of these. Figure 5 presents assumed results. (The problem of estimating the results of such expenditures is discussed in Chapter 4.)

To estimate the effects of different expenditures for additional salespeople, advertising and customer service, it is important to measure the right thing—the additions to total sales that would result from increments in these expenditures. For example, if the firm is already spending at the rate of $500,000 per year for advertising, one would estimate the effect of spending an additional $50,000, $100,000, etc. In the hypothetical example described in Figure 5, the increase in sales resulting from a $50,000

Unit Sales Increase from Added Outlays

Incremental Outlays (in $ thousands)	More Salespeople (unit sales)	More Advertising (unit sales)	Better Customer Service (unit sales)
50	600	500	450
100	1,150	1,000	900
150	1,650	1,500	1,300
200	2,100	1,900	1,600
250	2,500	2,200	1,800
300	2,800	2,350	1,900
350	3,200	2,400	1,950

Figure 5.   A simplified illustration of the equimarginal principle

increase in advertising would be 500 units. For an additional outlay of $50,000 for advertising, sales would increase another 500 units. With the estimates just given, management can calculate how best to allocate its funds between adding salesforce, more advertising and better customer service by applying the following rules:

1.   Do not make expenditures that add less to net income than the firm's target rate of return. (If the expenditure of $100,000 is estimated to yield a net profit of $12,000 and management has set a target rate of return on its investments of 15%, the expenditure should not be made.)

2.   Divide the budget so that the last dollar spent on any one of the three alternatives will yield the same number of added sales.

By following these two steps, one is applying the equimarginal principle. If this is done, a shift of funds from one use to another would reduce total sales, meaning the firm will achieve more sales by spending its funds in this way than by any other division of outlays.

To achieve that result involves some calculations but they are simple arithmetic once one estimates the sales increase that would result from alternative expenditures. Given the assumed facts in Figure 5, the best allocation of $450,000 in added outlays to increase sales among the three uses for funds would be $200,000 for added sales-force, $150,000 to increase advertising and $100,000 to improve customer service.

The Hierarchy of Objectives
as a Planning Tool

A hierarchy of objectives maps an organization's activities. It indicates the goals pursued, activities taken and alternatives considered. When this information is put in a structured form it orients senior members of a firm and gives them direction for their efforts. It communicates to all about the activities of everyone. It aids coordination and exposes any lack of coordination. In all of these ways, a hierarchy assists those who prepare a business plan and may be considered a specialized business plan.

A major benefit that planners derive from a hierarchy of objectives is that it suggests different goals that might be served by a single action program. For example, a firm can advertise to increase the support it receives from its retailers and distributors as well as to improve the firm's brand image among consumers. One can conduct training programs to improve productivity, create closer personal relations among members of the staff and increase loyalty to the firm. Planners who are aware of the firm's many instrumental goals are encouraged to devise actions that achieve more than one objective. As a minimum, they can look for actions that would reinforce the programs carried out by other members of the firm.

Hierarchies can and should be developed for lower levels of the firm and for subsidiaries by using the same means-end logic. Figure 2 presented a sample hierarchy for a firm's product design operation. The ultimate objectives were the same as instrumental objectives in the firm's hierarchy.

Conclusion

A hierarchy of objectives is a powerful management tool, but is valuable only if constructed with great care. A hierarchy of objectives for a firm structures its activities and gives the company a clear direction. It is an excellent tool for auditing the firm's problems and opportunities. Executives involved in the construction of a hierarchy of objectives receive valuable executive training.

In addition, a hierarchy of objectives can help in identifying and reconciling conflicting objectives. It also provides a framework for the application of the equimarginal principle to achieve an efficient allocation of limited resources. It helps guard against the common error of getting locked into a low-level objective.

II.

MODELS FOR EXECUTIVE DECISIONS

T O DO ANY JOB WELL, people must understand what they are doing. To repair an appliance, one needs to know how it works—what the key parts are, the functions they perform and how they fit together. To operate a business, one must understand the connection between the actions one takes and the consequences that follow. Fortunately, complete understanding is not needed for most tasks, but misunderstanding can be badly damaging.

Everyone has beliefs about most subjects. We all have conscious views about human motivation, how the government operates, how to deal with a cold, etc. These beliefs about how things work largely determine our decisions and actions.

Unfortunately, we have many unconscious beliefs that have great power over our behavior. Consequently, few of the models governing our actions are based on careful study and reflection. As a result, they are likely to be only partially correct and could be seriously flawed. Faulty beliefs, both conscious and unconscious, rather than limited information, explain most poor decisions and misguided actions.

Like everyone else, business executives hold many unexamined views about business. While some of them rest on a solid foundation, some do not and may be wrong. When executives' views are valid, their decisions are likely to be correct; when they are false, executives can only make correct decisions by chance.

Executives rarely are required to explain and defend their beliefs. They mainly rely upon their impressions, their intuition and personal experience and take their assumptions for granted. If their views are invalid, they will not be challenged since they are not expressed.

What has been referred to as "views," "understanding," "assumptions" and "beliefs" are unexplicit or unconscious *models*. On the other hand, some models of business phenomena are explicit and were developed with great care. Mainly, these appear in the business literature and especially in the writings of specialists in managerial economics, operations research, accounting and industrial organization. Those models are not necessarily valid, but they have been developed painstakingly and evaluated by specialists in their field. The number of models of business processes has increased steadily.

Valid models are extremely valuable intellectual tools. They convey and embody basic understanding of and insight into complicated phenomena. Such understanding enables executives to know what information to collect and how to interpret it. Facts alone usually are ambiguous and bewildering.

What Are Models?

Models are simplified replications of reality. A model expresses what we mean when we say that we know how something works, whether it be advertising, bonuses, a cannon, a FAX machine or a microwave oven. The chief characteristics of models are: (1) they simplify complex reality by stripping away nonessentials, (2) they include the essential elements, and, (3) they indicate the relationships among the component parts. The main purpose of models is to make clear something that is complicated. Their value depends upon the extent to which they increase understanding.

One can create different models of the same phenomenon. The form they take–verbal, mathematical, geometric, graphic, metaphorical, etc.–will depend upon the use to which they are put and the audience for which they are intended.

Models underlie all thinking. Only by following rules blindly can one act without an implicit model. By relying upon models that are not explicit, one runs the risk of serious error. When executives are asked to describe their assumptions about how some business process works, they usually find their response unconvincing even to themselves.

An Illustrative Model

A simple example will clarify this discussion. Figure 6a indicates the essence of all kinds of inventory problems. Firms hold inventories of raw materials, components, fin-

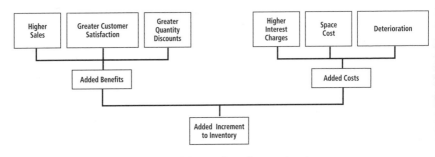

6a. *Gains and losses from increasing inventory*

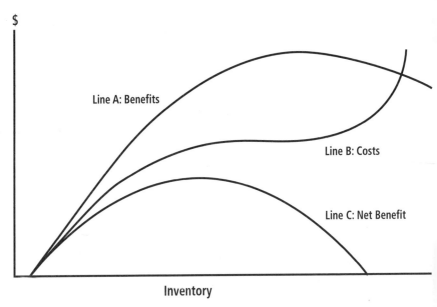

6b. *Opposing costs and finding the optimum inventory*

Figure 6. *A simple inventory model*

ished goods, labor, management, funds, machinery, etc., and the inventory model helps executives decide how much to hold of all of those things. By increasing inventory, the firm incurs certain costs. It also gains certain benefits. The task is to balance the costs and the gains to find the point that gives the greatest net benefits. Figure 6a indicates the basic logic of the model showing it consists of opposing costs—the costs of having too much or too little of something. Figure 6b translates the costs and benefits into concrete dollar amounts to derive a solution for a hypothetical example. Figure 6a, although very simple, makes obvious the main elements to be considered in making inventory decisions.

Since each business firm and each industry is unique to a substantial degree, executives would benefit from creating explicit models to meet their special needs. These models will ordinarily be quite complex but still very clear to executives familiar with the business.

With a little application and practice, business executives (or members of their staff) can create models of business processes that embody their understanding. Business experience, discussions with colleagues, formal training and reading of the business press account for most executives' understanding of their jobs. They already possess unexplicit models. With practice and guidance, they can make their understanding explicit and in the process learn a great deal. They will learn what they know and what they do not—and what deserves more thought.

How to Develop Models

To develop an explicit model, people must first try to set down their current views. To start the process, it generally is useful to create a checklist. Specifically, one would set down the things that come to mind relevant to a certain phenomenon. The list can be quite long and highly disorganized, including all the things that seem to be relevant.

The next step would be to group the items in the checklist, eliminating duplications. The third step is probably the most difficult. It consists of deciding how the grouped items relate to one another; that is, how the different elements fit together and form a process.

One way of creating a coherent structure out of the grouped items is to put them in one of the structures used to depict models. One such structure indicates the dependent and independent variables and thus indicates what one seeks to explain (the *dependent variables*) and identifies the main factors that influence them (the *independent variables*). See Figure 7. This model is simple and not very illuminating, but represents a large step forward when one's understanding is rudimentary. Models reflect the level of the model-maker's understanding.

Unit Sales is a function of:	**Personal Sales**
	Advertising
	Distribution Strength
	Relative Price
	Marketing Mix
	GNP

Figure 7. A dependent/independent variable model of unit sales

An Input-Output Model

An input-output model can be constructed from the grouped items on your checklist. Such a model identifies: (1) input, that is, items that are required to create the desired output, (2) output, which is the result desired, and (3) an indication of how the inputs are processed to create the output. It is easy to see that such a model might be developed for the production of some product, with inputs being raw materials, components, power, labor and management and the output being products of desired quality and quantity. The various productive processes that operate on the inputs would also be described by the model. This model can be applied to highly diverse phenomena. The author developed and applied such a model to great advantage to analyze the operations of a university. The effort to describe a university in input-output terms raised very useful questions about the source of university students and how one might better prepare students for university study. It also directed attention to measures that would improve the employability of the graduates by business, commerce and government.

Let us apply these three steps to a simplified example: What model might an executive construct to explain the effects of advertising in his or her industry?

The executive's checklist might include such things as:

1. Media that might be used.

2. Specific messages that might be communicated.

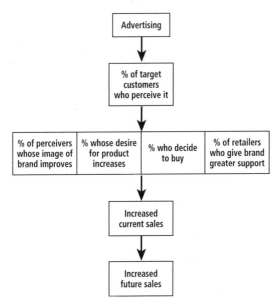

Figure 8.   A linear/sequential model of advertising's effects

3.   The information to transmit to potential customers.

4.   The target populations for the advertising.

5.   The desired effect on ultimate customers, distributors and retailers.

6.   A list of affordable electronic and print media.

7.   The effect of advertising on brand image, customer loyalty, etc.

This is a much shorter list than an executive would make in a concrete situation.

How might the executive organize these factors? Some items relate to the communicator (the firm), and other items refer to the instruments of communication (the media). And still other items deal with the message to be communicated or the target of the communication.

How then can the different parts be organized into a structure that is illuminating? One structure would be linear—it would show the business, then the media, then the message and then the targets of the message. (See Figure 8.) Another structure would be a simple dependent/independent variable model. It would look like Figure 7, which shows unit sales as the dependent variable and lists a number of independent variables which determine unit sales.

The executive presumably wants to create a structure that indicates how advertising works in the company's market. We assume that the executive believes advertising exerts its greatest effect on retailers by providing them with factual information. Its secondary effect is on the ultimate consumer by strengthening the brand image of the product and giving reassurance about its quality.

The executive may also usefully structure these views of how advertising works in the company's business in quantitative form. One question might be whether sales will increase in direct proportion to advertising expenditures. Familiarity with the business literature should lead to the recognition of a very common relationship between the input of advertising dollars and the output of unit sales. It takes the form of a modified "J" curve. (See Figure 9.) Up to some threshold, advertising has no effect on sales; beyond that threshold, it increases sales slowly. At

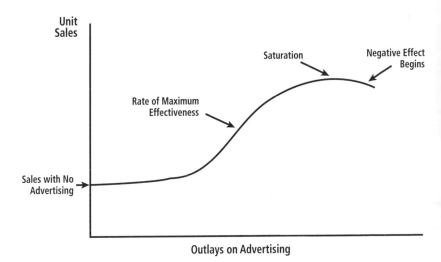

Figure 9. A model of a typical relationship between inputs and outputs

some point, as expenditures are increased, sales are likely to rise rapidly up to some level. Beyond that level of outlay, sales respond less to advertising expenditures. At some point, advertising will no longer increase sales—a point of saturation would have been reached. Expenditures beyond that point might actually reduce sales by antagonizing some customers.

This geometric model is extremely illuminating because it suggests some of the factors that influence the effectiveness of advertising. It is extremely simple in form, and it invites quantification. Specifically, it challenges the executive to determine the level of advertising required to exceed the threshold, what level achieves the highest pay-off and the amount of expenditure that approaches saturation. (Those points would differ with different messages, targets and media.) In addition, it represents an antidote to the common assumption that sales increase in direct proportion to advertising outlays.

Other Models of Business Processes

Several very general and valuable structural models deal with the production process and logistics. These are essentially work-scheduling models. PERT is a relatively complex model which describes specific production processes in a manner that highlights likely bottlenecks. Again, these models can and should be custom-tailored to the needs of individual firms and elaborated to incorporate special circumstances.

Another pair of simple models has extremely wide application. These are the *causal net* and *consequence net* models. These models stress that every phenomenon has more than one cause and more than one consequence. Moreover, each cause itself has antecedent causes and each consequence has consequences of its own. Figure 10 expresses these concepts graphically. Both models are combined in Figure 11 to explain the causes for and effects of price changes. These models push decision makers to search out nonobvious causes and effects and deter them from assuming that their actions have a single cause or effect.

These two models can be combined with another model termed the *parties to the process*. This model implies that several important parties are likely to be affected by any decision and a decision-maker should take account of

A. Causes for increases in advertising

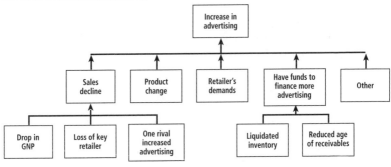

B. Consequences of adding a new product

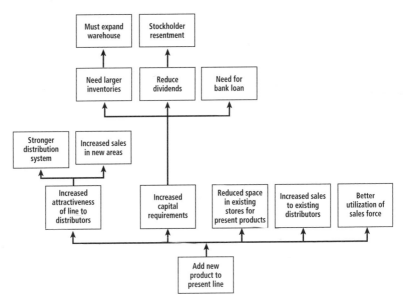

Figure 10.   The causal and consequences net models

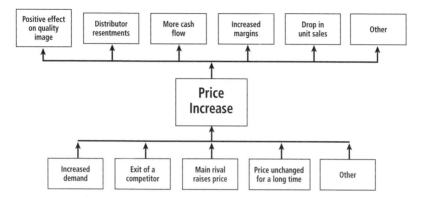

Figure 11.   The causal and consequence net models combined

the effect of a decision on each of those parties. For example, business decisions often affect ultimate customers, distributors, retailers, competitors and employees. Another example taken from academia would be decisions by college presidents that affect students, faculty, administrators, potential donors and accreditation agencies. Other models of use to business appear at many points in this book.

Suggestions for Executive Action

What then are executives to do about models once they recognize their vital importance? In serious conversation, and after reading an important article, it is helpful to put the useful ideas presented into the form of an explicit model. Three actions are fairly clear:

1.   Executives should study existing models of business processes. That involves becoming familiar

with descriptions of models that are described in the literature.

2.   They should produce, or have developed for them, models that incorporate the special features of the major facets of their business.

3.   When making important decisions, they should make explicit their now-held models.

A Nonbusiness Example

Businesspeople are not the only ones who base many of their decisions on unconscious models. Writers of professional literature are another group—and this author is no exception. Like all students, I have been taught how to write good sentences, paragraphs and compositions—but not how to write articles and books. Having written some articles and books, I developed convictions, most of which are still unconscious, about what constitutes a good article and book.

After some reflection, the following thoughts came to mind. First, the title and opening paragraphs are crucial to attracting, informing and holding readers. They also strongly influence how much readers learn. But what constitutes a good title and opening paragraph?

The title should attract the kinds of readers I want and discourage those for whom I am not writing. It should be clear and yet "catchy," although these goals sometimes conflict.

What makes an ideal opening paragraph? In my view, it should be simple and descriptive of what is to follow, in general terms rather than in great detail. It should be spirited, and suggest pleasant surprises and conclusions of consequence.

Further reflection revealed my conviction that an article and book should resemble a vaudeville show: It should open "with a bang," that is, its start should be lively, upbeat, vigorous and full of promise. Its opening should mainly strive for emotional rather than cognitive impact. Thereafter, the various vaudeville acts (chapters) should skillfully present a parade of talent. Each act should end before the audience is sated. The final act should somehow tie the individual acts together and end on a high note. It was a surprise to learn that I believed there was an analogy between good writing and vaudeville. It was of particular surprise to learn that I have a view of what makes a successful vaudeville show.

This example has been carried far enough to indicate that one learns a great deal in the process of model building. Some of the results are surprising—many impressions that cannot be supported and issues that were never faced before come to the fore.

Summary and Conclusion

Top management mainly does the high-level abstract thinking for an organization. Its convictions, theories, impressions and opinions largely determine the validity of its decisions. In other words, executives are about as good as their models—especially those that relate to their interaction with colleagues and subordinates. If they recognize this fairly obvious conclusion, executives will try to learn the models that have been developed by specialists in business and learn how to develop models that apply specifically to their job responsibilities.

III.

Costs

E CONOMISTS MAKE THEIR GREATEST contribution
to business executives in the area of costs. Mainly
they provide an antidote for some cost accounting
doctrines. Economists' and accountants' views of costs
differ, sometimes dramatically.

Cost Estimates

Accurate forecasts of costs and revenues are crucial for
economic efficiency. Consequently, all business actions are,
or should be, strongly influenced by cost computations.
Executives' estimates of what they must give up to carry
out some action—whether to produce, transport, store,
finance, advertise, research or sell something—determine
whether the action should be taken. Unless they measure
costs accurately, they may conduct activities that yield less
income than they cost or may consider as unprofitable
some opportunities that, in reality, are profitable.

Consequently, executives require accurate cost
estimates. To estimate costs accurately they need valid
concepts as much as they need facts. Much controversy

surrounds the question of what items to include in costs and what items to exclude. Most executives' views of costs are similar to those of accountants, which are not appropriate for decision making purposes.

What Are Costs?

Costs involve sacrifices. Sacrifices result from outlays and actions that work against achieving a firm's goals. Anything that injures an individual or an organization is a cost whether or not it involves an outlay of funds. Cost is also different from and usually larger than the price paid. Most purchases involve costs of time, inconvenience, outlays to contact the place of purchase, payment for transport, sales taxes, possibly a credit charge and other costs incurred as a result of the purchase.

What Are the True Costs of a Decision?

To the question, what should executives include in costs when making a decision, economists offer a simple answer: the relevant costs are *decision* or *action* costs. These are costs that would not be incurred if the decision were not made. More specifically, the cost of doing something is the increase in total cost that results from doing it. This answer differs conceptually from the traditional accounting answer of *standard* or *full cost*—and it often results in substantially different measures of cost.

Decision theorists coined the concept of *decision cost*. As the name suggests, the decision cost is the estimated actual change in cost that results from carrying out a decision. It is the increase in total costs that results from making a particular decision under specified circumstances.

To measure decision cost one computes the difference between what the firm's total costs would be if it made the decision and if it did not. If total costs to make 1,000 widgets were $10,000 and it cost $10,005 to make 1,001 widgets, the decision cost of the last widget would be $5.

Economists stress that costs are situational. They depend upon the conditions prevailing when the decision is carried out. Given that relevant conditions change with some frequency, cost forecasts must take them into account. For that reason, one cannot assert that the cost of, say, a specific machine tool–a given model of a specific brand–is X dollars. The cost of such a machine tool depends upon where, when, how, etc., it will be produced, transported, prepared for sale and so on.

For example, labor costs are much higher than usual when a plant works overtime and, paradoxically, also when output is below capacity. Some failure of machinery can cause costs to soar, even as breakdowns of transportation can raise costs. Hence, the conclusion that there is no such thing as the cost of anything. Items produced on the same assembly line on the same day may have different costs.

Costs result mainly from decisions which lead to actions but also from consciously deciding not to act. The relevant costs for executives–the ones that should determine what they do–are the cost estimates made at the time of decision. Accounting costs report history–the result of past decisions. These accounting costs cannot be changed and are not subject to decision.

Executives' interests in costs are not abstract and theoretical. They want to know the costs (monetary and nonmonetary) that they will incur to make particular decisions and take particular actions. Consequently, past costs and costs in general are not relevant to their decisions.

While the concept of decision costs is very simple, business executives encounter many different cost terms and measures that can be bewildering. If they concentrate on only those costs that are relevant to the decisions at hand, they can avoid serious error. Remember almost all the cost figures they see are prepared by accountants and record past events–and as such, are not appropriate for current decision making. Decisions should be based on future costs.

The Accounting Vocabulary

An extensive accounting vocabulary describes different facets of costs. Most cost terms are descriptive and indicate the specific purpose for which funds were spent. Labor costs, cost of materials, supplies, professional service costs, capital costs, repairs, etc., are examples. Other terms, like *fixed* and *variable* costs, describe how costs vary with changes in output. (Accountants also distinguish between fixed overhead and variable overhead.) Other terms are used to indicate whether particular costs can be attributed to specific products–these are *direct* costs. Overhead is an *indirect* cost, because it cannot be assigned to a specific product. Some cost terms refer to the manner in which one describes costs–as total amounts, as averages or as increments to total costs. One cannot discuss costs from any perspective without using these accounting terms. None of these accounting terms are the same as decision costs.

When one estimates the cost of a particular decision, these accounting terms acquire a new meaning. Decision labor costs represent additions to total labor cost that will result from the decision in question. Average or standard costs are always irrelevant if one is estimating the cost of a specific decision. Decision makers should only be concerned with how a specific action would affect the firm's total costs under the conditions that are expected to prevail. This figure should be the basis for their decision.

The Cost Vocabulary of Economists

Managerial economists and decision theorists employ a very simple cost vocabulary. Costs are either decision costs or irrelevant costs. *Sunk* costs (discussed presently) are one type of irrelevant cost that is frequently included in cost estimates. *Decision* costs are whatever outlays or other sacrifices (especially intangible costs) result from a particular decision.

Figure 12 defines the most common and important accounting and decision theory cost terms.

The Computation of Decision Costs

As stressed earlier, decision costs are influenced by the particular conditions under which the decision is carried out. Consequently, to estimate decision costs one must specify in considerable detail what action is contemplated—when, how, by whom, etc.—and under what conditions. Once

Accounting Terms

Fixed/Variable Costs	Indicate whether costs are affected by changes in output
Direct/Indirect Costs	Indicate whether costs can be assigned to specific products
Standard Costs	A special calculation of costs per unit at a standard sales volume
Full Costs	Similar to standard costs; include both fixed and variable costs
Overhead Costs	Indicate total nonvariable costs; synonymous with fixed costs
Total/Average/Unit Costs	Indicate different methods of expressing cost data

Economic Terms

Decision Costs (also relevant and incremental costs)	The change in total cost resulting from a particular decision
Opportunity Cost	The income given up to carry out a particular decision
Sunk Costs	Past outlays that cannot be reduced
Programmed Costs (also optional costs)	Costs not needed to produce/sell but incurred to reduce other costs or to increase revenue. Examples are costs of advertising, research, promotion, public relations, etc.

Figure 12. Meaning of key cost terms

executives recognize what is to be done under specified conditions, they can estimate the different negative effects of the contemplated actions and assign monetary values to them. They should not be concerned solely with dollar outlays or accounting charges. Often, costs are intangibles—items that injure the firm but are not even recorded by accountants.

Intangible costs mainly represent injuries to the firm—effects that reduce revenue or increase money costs in the future. They also include *opportunity* costs (discussed presently), also not recorded by accountants. Conversely, decision costs would not include some items that accountants include in costs like overhead and depreciation.

A Case Study

A lengthy hypothetical example will highlight the difference between accounting and economic costs. Our purpose is to make clear the valuable concepts of: decision costs, sunk costs, opportunity costs and intangible costs.

For our example, several assumptions will simplify these basic ideas. First, we assume that the costs of labor, materials, equipment, space, power, etc. remain constant throughout the life of the enterprise. Second, we assume that the quality of the product and technology does not change over the firm's life.

We start with Mr. Jones who has had many years of experience in framus manufacturing and is deciding whether to set up his own firm. After some research, he decides to explore the advisability of creating a firm with the capacity to produce around 40,000 framuses annually. He knows that his costs will be different from those of established producers (whose costs he knows approximately). He also realizes that his unit costs will be higher during the first year or two of operation than they will be in subsequent years. He expects his sales and costs to vary from year to year.

Jones' decision to establish a framus firm involves three separate estimates of cost. First, he must estimate his cost to acquire the resources (mainly land, plant, machinery and equipment) needed by an enterprise that can efficiently produce and sell 40,000 units annually and second, the start-up costs he will incur before the firm produces any revenue. Third, and most important, he wants to estimate his costs if he decides to produce approximately 40,000 framuses annually. The answer to these questions will determine Jones' decision.

Mr. Jones recognizes that cost estimates cannot be exact, and they need not be for his purposes. Although appropriate for scientists, complete precision is an unreasonable goal for business executives.

Mr. Jones' Capital Requirements

Jones must acquire many things to enter the framus industry. These include such things as plant and land, machinery of different types, material handling equipment, trucks and office equipment. These assets are necessary expenditures to carry out a decision to establish a framus business. The cost of those assets does not represent a cost of the firm's output until production begins, but is a cost of the decision to enter the business. We will assume that Jones estimates the cost of those assets to be $700,000, and that he can obtain credit (via mortgage and bank loans) of $600,000 to acquire them.

Mr. Jones' Start-up Costs

In addition to requiring physical plant and equipment, Jones must create a management team and a labor force before he begins production. He will also need *working capital* to pay for materials, components, and his workers and managers during the shake-down period. More-

Capital costs:

Land and building	$500,000	
Machinery and equipment	200,000	
Total capital costs		$700,000

Opportunity costs:

Foregone income from job	$75,000	
1st year interest on Jones' investment	30,000	
Total opportunity costs	105,000	

Other start-up costs:

Introductory advertising	45,000	
Professional services	30,000	
Interest on working capital	2,500	
First year's inefficiencies	15,000	
Total other start-up costs	92,500	
Total start-up costs		$197,500
Total capital requirements		**$897,500**

Figure 13. Costs to establish the framus business

over, he believes that he must employ an advertising agency, a marketing research firm, a public relations person and the services of an attorney who will perform services before the firm produces any income. Jones will also need to *carry* some accounts receivable, since no firms in the framus industry sell for cash. All of these items involve monetary outlays before he will obtain any revenue from sales and must be arranged if the business is to be formed.

Mr. Jones estimates that he would be required to devote one year, full time, to set up the production facilities, create a management team and workforce and do the other things required before the firm produces income. As a result, he would incur a sizeable *opportunity cost*–to be explained presently. In addition, Jones would incur such start-up costs as interest on his mortgage, insurance on his production and office equipment and other minor start-up costs.

Thus, a decision to establish the business would require Jones to incur many one-time, non-recurring costs. Unless the firm makes sufficient profits after it begins operations to defray these as well as its subsequent operating costs, Jones should not establish the business.

If Jones could borrow funds to meet all of his needs– a highly unlikely event–his personal capital requirements would be zero. On the other hand, if he must pay cash for everything he required before producing revenue, his capital requirements would be extremely high.

Opportunity Costs

Opportunity costs are confusing, partly because they do not involve any expenditure–they are not even recorded in a firm's accounting records. Rather they represent a loss of income that results from foregoing, or doing without, income that would be otherwise obtained. In this hypothetical case, included is what Jones could earn if he accepted a position with an established firm as well as the return he could earn on the $300,000 of his personal funds invested in the business. These are sums that Jones could get if he did not establish his own firm. They represent concrete sacrifices that Jones must make to establish a framus business and are real costs of the decision to set up his own business.

We assume that Jones knows that he can get a position that would pay $75,000 in salary and fringe benefits. Another cost to be included is the income he estimates he would earn on the $300,000 he must withdraw from savings and invest in the business. He estimates the latter to be $30,000 before taxes.

These opportunity costs deserve a closer look for they involve a type of cost that is often overlooked or computed incorrectly. Recognize at the outset that opportunity costs do not appear anywhere in accounting records.

Let us examine a few other examples of opportunity cost sacrifices that result when a firm does something that prevents it from doing something else of value. For example, a firm that makes an acquisition instead of entering the European market sacrifices the returns it would have made on its European operation. Consequently, that lost income should be included in the decision cost of the acquisition. Similarly, if a firm accepts a contract for its services that will net it a profit of $100,000 when it could have obtained $120,000 for similar services from another customer, it is incurring an opportunity loss of $20,000.

Clearly, such opportunity costs are very real and are costs of decisions that prevent the firm from taking other actions. It is likely that opportunity costs are often overlooked by decision-makers. However, outsiders will never know because, as indicated, they are not recorded in a firm's financial records.

One can be certain that decision-makers select what they consider the best opportunity of which they are aware. Consequently, their decisions yield more anticipated profit than the known alternatives. However, they may make a variety of errors involving opportunity costs. First, they may not take account of better opportunities that may arise if one waits. Future opportunities that are foreclosed by a decision are costs of that decision.

A common error involving opportunity costs results from using accounting costs to measure the value of assets and services that the firm possesses. This error is illustrated by another hypothetical example. A manager of a consulting firm receives a request for the services of a particular member of the firm from a regular client. That consultant's salary and fringes cost the firm $11,000 per month. Since the assignment would last six months, the "accounting cost" for the consultant's services would be $66,000. The client would pay $100,000 for his services.

These facts suggest that the manager should be happy to assign the consultant to that client. However, it happens that the particular consultant is supervising several difficult and lucrative projects, which he could not manage if he took this new assignment. If he were taken off his present assignments, the CEO estimates that the firm's costs would rise by $40,000 over the six months and income would decline by $80,000. The cost of shifting him from his present duties to the client would be $120,000 plus $66,000—far more than the client would pay.

The important moral to this example is that one cannot take payments to employees (or the book value of assets) as measures of their value to the firm. To compute opportunity costs, one must estimate what employees (and assets) add to the firm's net income. One should expect most employees to produce more value for the firm than they are paid. If the reverse were true, the firm would lose money by employing them.

As indicated, opportunity costs arise when one action makes it impossible to take other valuable actions. Such foreclosure occurs when either time or resources are not sufficient to exploit all attractive alternatives. Mr. Jones could not both start the new enterprise and take a position that would pay $75,000. If he invested funds in the new venture, he could not earn $30,000 in interest and dividends on other investments. Likewise, the consultant whose services were required by the new assignment would not have been able to continue to manage the lucrative projects on which he was engaged. These examples suggest that opportunity costs are common. Moreover, they represent sacrifices no less genuine than outlays of cash and should be included in estimates of decision costs.

Most substantial decisions involve opportunity costs since few firms have unlimited resources. A decision to do something usually means that the firm must give up any alternative. In practice, that means that management will forego the alternatives of which it is aware. But, what of the attractive alternatives available that management has not identified?

This vital question raises the issue of how long and how painstakingly management should search for attractive alternatives before making a major move. How thoroughly should one search for some better alternative before settling for one course of action? We know no good answer to this important question. However, one rule that has been proposed is that one should never select between two alternatives—like "go" or "no go"—but always consider at least *three* alternatives.

Other Costs to Consider

Before leaving the issue of opportunity costs, mention should be made of two costs that are almost universally miscalculated. These are the cost of a firm's existing plant and equipment and the cost of undistributed profits. Neither of these is reported in a firm's accounting records. Both involve the use of assets which could produce income if devoted to some other use than the firm actually makes of them. While one might disagree about the value to be placed on these costs, no doubt can exist about the fact that they are legitimate costs that should be assigned to the products that are made with them. These are well-described as "hidden costs" (Maital, 1994).

Let us now return to Jones' decision to start a framus business. We have discussed his capital requirements and his start-up costs. Because Jones can borrow $600,000, he is able to cover his capital requirements. However, he must pay interest on his borrowings. And in making his decision to enter the framus business, he needs to consider the opportunity cost on the $300,000 he must invest in the enterprise. Figure 13 showed start-up costs of $197,500. Start-up costs must be carefully forecast and planned. Mr. Jones in reality will likely have start-up costs in addition to those listed. These expenditures add to Jones' start-up capital requirements. He must somehow arrange to acquire the listed assets and services.

Jones' Estimate of Costs to Make Framuses

To decide whether to establish a framus firm, Jones mainly wants to know his costs (and expected price) after the firm achieves its regular output level of around 40,000 units annually. It is from operations over the expected 20-year life of the enterprise that Jones would cover his investment, his start-up costs and the costs of producing framuses year in and out–plus produce a profit.

On an annual sales volume of around 40,000 units over the expected 20-year life of the enterprise–800,000 units– Jones' start-up costs are small. They represent a cost per framus of roughly 21 cents.

Observe that Jones included in his start-up costs a return on his investment of $300,000. Jones predicts that he will be able to withdraw his entire investment from profits within his first five years of operations. This assumption influences the cost of starting the business as well as the cost of continuing a personal investment in the company. (We can assume that Jones could liquidate the business, or sell it, and get most of his investment back.)

Jones' Costs After He Starts Operations

The decision costs to produce framuses are very different from those to establish the firm. Figure 14 presents Mr. Jones' estimate of his costs to produce framuses once the firm has achieved sales of around 40,000 units– which he expects it to do within three years. Given these assumed estimates and his forecast that he would obtain a price of at least $175 for each framus, Jones clearly would elect to enter the business. His estimated decision costs for entering the business include overhead and amount to $128.95 per unit (see Figure 14), substantially below the price he expects. He could easily defray his start-up costs from a business that sold 40,000 units annually that cost $128.95 each and sold at a price of $175. Over a 20-year

	Total	Per Unit
Non-product costs (general overhead)		
Managerial salaries	$360,000	$9.00
Ins., office, misc.	80,000	2.00
Marketing costs	20,000	0.50
Interest on working capital	8,000	0.20
Interest on Jones' investment	(30,000 declining to zero in 5 years)	
Total Overhead Cost (excludes interest on Jones' investment)	$468,000	$11.70

	Total	Per Unit
Product Costs		
Production labor	$1,600,000	$40.00
Materials and components	1,800,000	45.00
Supplies and power	400,000	10.00
Sales force's commissions	600,000	15.00
Depreciation and maintenance	240,000	6.00
Contingencies	50,000	1.25
Total Product Cost	$4,690,000	$117.25
Total	$5,158,000	$128.95

Figure 14.   Jones' accounting costs after starting production (for output of 40,000 units)

period, he would earn a profit of $46.05 on 800,000 units—a total of $36,840,000. This profit is above Mr. Jones' annual salary of $65,000 which is included in the firm's costs.

Mr. Jones is confident that his cost and profit estimates are quite reliable because a large percentage of his costs are variable and vary in rough proportion to output.

As described in Figure 14, overhead would be less than 10 percent of total costs with sales of 40,000 units per year.

Jones' Decision Costs Under Different Circumstances

Let us explore several potential developments that would affect Jones' business to see how each would affect decision costs and compare those costs with accounting costs. First, we will assume that three years after he established the business, Jones' sales were only 20,000 units. What would be his decision costs to produce framuses at that level of sales? How would he reason about a decision to leave the business?

As indicated earlier, the unit total costs would be the same as his costs if sales were 40,000 units. The difference would be small because the firm has a relatively low overhead. But for decision costs on producing framuses we are not concerned with overhead. For the decision to enter the business, decision costs include overhead. For a production decision, only product costs are considered. Overhead costs are not affected by the decision. So, at a sales volume of 20,000 units, Jones' unit decision costs would be only a little more than $117.25, any increase accounted for by product costs that are not directly variable, such as depreciation. At both sales volumes, overhead costs are not included in decision costs because they are assumed to be unaffected by changes in sales volume. Accounting costs per unit include overhead; at sales of 20,000 overhead costs per unit would be double those at a 40,000 sales volume. Jones' decision costs per unit are stable. His total decision costs would vary in proportion to his output.

Even if Jones' sales declined to 5,000 units, the per-unit cost of a decision to produce framuses would remain the same. However, accounting costs would reflect changes in unit overhead cost. They would be one-eighth as great if sales were 40,000 units as at a sales volume of 5,000. Since standard costs usually are estimated for a standard output, they would not change even with very large changes in sales. None of Jones' overhead costs would enter into his decision costs for they would be virtually unaffected by the amount he decided to produce.

We have assumed, fairly realistically that Jones' overhead costs would not change markedly even if he sold far less than he expected—for a short period. We should consider whether overhead costs—and all fixed costs—are really fixed. Are they entirely beyond Jones' control? Can Jones realistically reduce any of his overhead costs and by how much? Could he liquidate some of his equipment? Might he rent out some of his plant and office space? Could he discharge some of his office help? Could he lower his insurance coverage and cost? These questions invite a discussion of sunk costs and indicate an important difference between sunk and overhead (fixed) costs.

Sunk Costs

Sunk costs are costs already incurred that cannot be changed. They are similar to fixed costs in many respects but different in one important aspect. As we just noted, fixed costs often can be reduced in time. That is not true of sunk costs. More important, almost every manager understands how overhead costs are affected by changes in sales volume but many fail to deal logically with sunk costs. As will be explained, emotional factors make it difficult for most people to ignore sunk costs.

Consider the case of a pharmaceutical firm that spent $3 million on research to develop a drug they estimated would yield a net profit of over $1.5 million—after covering research costs. However, the research did not succeed. Management then considered another research project of equal cost to develop the same drug, capitalizing on what was learned in the earlier project. Management decided against the project because a combined cost of $6 million could not be recovered if the research were successful.

Since the firm could earn profits of $1.5 million above research cost, the second research project would appear to be highly attractive. The decision cost of the second project is only $3 million and not $6 million. The first project's research cost is irrelevant—it is irretrievable. By including the unsuccessful $3 million research expenditure, the firm would give up an opportunity to make a net profit of $1.5 million.

Mr. Jones also has sunk costs. Most of his very considerable start-up costs are sunk and cannot be recovered. If his plant and equipment could not be sold, their costs are sunk.

The most general type of sunk cost is the cost of an asset. Once the transaction is completed for its purchase, the cost of the asset is irrelevant to its future sale. One might get much more than was paid for it on resale or may, under some circumstances, be forced to pay someone to take it away. Many people find it emotionally painful to accept less for an asset than they paid (or less than its book value). That feeling can lead them to hold onto assets until their value falls even more. Conversely, many people are happy to sell assets for a little more than they paid for them, even though their intrinsic value is far more. As these examples indicate, sunk costs can reflect strong psychological feelings against acknowledging past mistakes. In some cases, they result in a firm's including costs that are irrelevant—in others, they lead people to throw away good money after bad.

Intangibles

Several references have already been made to intangible costs. These are a major consideration for management because they often are large in size and pose vexing problems. Not much is known about how such costs are treated currently by most executives. A fairly common practice is to acknowledge that they exist, to identify what they are and then to ignore them in one's calculations. That policy treats intangibles as if they represented zero costs.

At the opposite extreme, some executives faced with major intangibles conclude that they cannot undertake any action that will have those intangible costs. That policy treats intangibles as if they represented costs of infinity.

The fact is that intangible costs are neither zero nor infinitely large. They must be valued at some specific monetary figure, even while recognizing that such a figure is likely to be incorrect. Executives should ask what is the negative value of specific intangible costs? To be meaningful, this issue requires a discussion of specific examples.

Intangible costs take many forms. The most important and common are damages to employee morale, a worsening of relations among members of top management, reductions in worker loyalty, declines in brand image, losses of strong distributors and a decline in retailers' confidence in the integrity of the firm. Proof that these intangibles are very valuable consists of the fact that businesses spend so much to prevent these things from occurring. That fact suggests how executives can place a concrete monetary value on them in decision situations.

Let us consider the problem of a CEO faced with a recommendation that is estimated to increase the firm's profits between $1.5 and $ 2.2 million during the next year alone. The V.P. Marketing strongly opposes the proposal on the grounds that it would alienate many loyal distributors. The V.P.'s view is, "Our most important asset is a strong distributor organization. It took us 20 years to create our present distributor set up and we shouldn't do anything to injure it."

In many situations, the program would be rejected by the CEO on the basis of that statement alone. If so, he will have assigned a cost of infinity (or at least $1.5 to $2.2 million) to the damage to distributor loyalty. On the other hand, if he ignored what the V.P. Marketing said, he would value the cost at zero. Both positions are irrational. The challenge to executives in such situations is to find a method of placing a reasonable value on the intangible cost.

The following recommendation by the V.P. Finance suggests a way out of the dilemma, "Consider actions that we could take to undo any damage to the distributor's loyalty. There must be things we could do that would build loyalty?" For example, the company could guarantee prompter delivery of supplies, easier repair service, easier credit terms, etc. The cost of these programs is the maximum intangible damage that the program would cause.

This line of thinking requires the executive to estimate the cost of creating intangible benefits to offset the damage that will be done by the projected program. Presumably the CEO or the Marketing V.P. have frequently faced the question of how much effort and cost the firm should expend to strengthen the distributor organization.

Conversely, if an executive must value an intangible benefit, he can ask how much the firm would be willing to pay—for advertising, public relations, product improvements, etc.—to gain such a benefit.

Although it is painful to estimate intangibles, executives do it in a different context and do not consider themselves to be placing a value on intangibles. Executives must recognize that their decisions mainly concern intangibles, which ultimately produce tangible results. It is therefore crucial that executives learn the different methods by which they might estimate the value of intangibles.

Significance of Managerial Cost Concepts

The value of the cost concepts developed by managerial economists does not consist simply of logical rigour. They are valuable because they lead to more profitable decisions and actions than one would reach on the basis of accounting costs.

Unfortunately, economists have mainly espoused the value of decision costing in the context of "marginal cost pricing." They point out, correctly, that the relevant costs for decisions to produce output are incremental costs. This notion is very relevant and helpful for regulatory bodies dealing with public utility rates. However, that concept can be destructive in unregulated markets, especially where overhead costs are high. The damage results from the false assumption that firms should base their prices on decision costs. Firms that base their prices on decision costs can, and generally do, depress prices and eliminate profits and cause numerous failures. Their error is to ignore the importance of demand and competition.

The chief benefits of decision costing are found in other applications, namely in dealing with the addition and deletion of activities. These include vertical integration, "make or buy" decisions, the addition of new products, new product features, entry into new geographic markets, etc. Decision costing revolves mainly about the cost implications of combining different productive activities. Proposals to add new activities often derive from the fact that most firms possess resources that are not fully utilized and can be put to use in a related activity. For example, a firm's sales force who calls upon hospitals to sell, say, a piece of medical equipment could add other items (by purchase) for its sales force to offer at a very low cost. Decision costs take account of synergies that are lost in accounting cost estimates and lead to the fuller utilization of a firm's resources.

All firms are unique in some significant respect, even if they operate in the same geographic market of the same industry. The addition of the same new product feature, new method of manufacturing, marketing, distribution, etc. would affect the costs of individual firms differently. Some would gain great synergistic cost benefits while others might actually suffer a cost disadvantage. The accounting costs for new activities are likely to be very similar for such firms, but their decision costs would vary widely.

Summary and Conclusions

Businesses are forced by tax law to measure costs, which represent a deduction for tax purposes. Accountants measure those costs according to government regulations even while exercising limited options. However, they act as historians in that capacity and measure past costs.

As stressed, management can do little about the past and must face the future in its decisions and actions. It relies on forecasts of the costs of its future actions. Executives require estimates of decision costs—the change in total costs that will result from their decisions. This cost concept is delightfully simple and clear and has no need for the large number of cost concepts one meets in the accounting literature.

The key cost concepts that managers must master are these: opportunity costs, sunk costs and intangible costs. These are not complicated but somehow "go against the grain" of many executives. They are uncomfortable with them because the field of cost computation has for centuries been the province of accountants who are basically historians rather than futurists. The most daunting task executives face in computing decision costs is to place a reasonable value on intangibles–both costs and benefits.

IV.

THE VALUATION OF
PROGRAMS AND ASSETS

E XECUTIVES RECEIVE MANY PROPOSALS that involve sizeable expenditures and must decide what they are worth. They also must place a value on physical assets when they purchase plant and equipment. In addition, most of their decisions require them to place a value on such intangible assets as brand loyalty, a strong executive team, good labor relations and so on. In addition, executives often must estimate the value that others place on their assets as in the case of distributors, bankers, investors and customers so that they can negotiate successfully with them. It will be shown that these decisions revolve primarily around estimates of benefits. Of course, they also call for accurate estimates of decision costs, a subject discussed in Chapter 3. To be successful, an executive clearly must be skilled at making evaluations.

To place a value on physical assets and to evaluate proposals that the firm take specific actions, decision-makers must do the following:

1. Forecast the effect of the asset or action on the firm's future net revenues

2. Adjust those forecasts to take account of risk and uncertainty

3. Place a current value on future revenues

4. Translate distributions of potential outcomes into a single value.

Perhaps most important of all, executives must select the methods by which they will carry out the preceding four steps.

Managerial economics and decision theory offer methods to deal with these difficult issues in a rigorous manner. They do not guarantee the best answers but promise to produce the best decisions possible under the circumstances. The methods described take time, effort, special skills and may impose substantial money costs. Some executives who are familiar with these methods know that they rest on assumptions that often cannot be met in full, so they rely on other methods that have no explicit or rational basis.

Fortunately, many of the proposals that executives evaluate clearly are worth so much more or less than their cost that no precise valuation is required. Decisions are easy in those cases. Also, with experience, executives develop shortcuts that reduce the cost and effort of making careful evaluations.

What Are Things Worth?

According to economic doctrine, things are worth whatever one can get for them. That view does not help much with the valuation of proposals for action, intangible assets and with tangible assets for which there is no active market. The market for many business assets is very imperfect; for instance, the price a firm would obtain for an asset if it had to sell within, say, three days would be far less than it could get in, say, three months. Unique items— objets d'art, antiques, unusual pieces of real estate—are clear examples of such markets that are familiar to almost everyone.

A firm's assets in the form of heavy machinery, specialized plant equipment and so on are other examples. If a firm is liquidating its plant and equipment under severe time pressure, it will usually get far less for them than if it sells them as part of an operating business. If the firm has a substantial amount of time to find buyers for its plant and equipment, it sometimes will come close to obtaining the replacement value of its assets. Thus, the value of tangible assets is strongly influenced by prevailing special circumstances.

In addition, such precious assets as strong channels of distribution, strong ties with suppliers, good relations with distributors, employee loyalty and a strong top management team have no market, except through sale or merger of the enterprise. However, these intangible assets are extremely valuable to management, owners and to some other firms. Indeed, top executives typically assert that their employees, their distributors, brand image, etc. are their most valuable assets.

Do Businesses Value
Their Assets Correctly?

How, then, do businesspeople place a financial value on the assets they now own? Isn't the typical firm's balance sheet a good enough measure of a firm's assets and liabilities?

The answer is no, balance sheets do not even attempt to measure the firm's most valuable assets. And, by knowing the true value of assets that are undervalued or not valued at all, executives' decisions will be based on more accurate information.

Since balance sheets do not place a value on intangible assets they may lead executives to ignore some of a firm's most precious resources. Moreover, balance sheets almost always undervalue the worth of successful enterprises. Similarly, to assess accurately the performance of a firm's management, one should measure the change in value of the firm's intangible and tangible assets.

A management team that creates a skilled, loyal and dedicated work force has created a precious asset. That asset should be assigned a reasonable monetary value if one is measuring the worth of the enterprise. Those responsible for creating such assets deserve rewards no less than others who, say, produce sales increases. Consequently, changes in the value of a firm's assets, tangible and intangible, should be combined with its financial returns to assess management's performance.

Firms can also have major intangible liabilities. A hostile union that poisons labor relations, a negative brand image, employees with long seniority and high pay scales who are members of a strong union all reduce the true value of a firm, but these are not reflected on its balance sheet. In time, financial reports of the firm—profit and loss statements as well as its balance sheets—will reflect the effects of both intangible assets and liabilities.

Many executives argue that they should not value intangible assets and liabilities because they cannot make accurate estimates. Some argue that since you cannot distribute intangibles to stockholders as dividends they therefore should be ignored. These arguments do not take account of the crucial fact that intangibles have value only if they produce future tangible effects. The same is true of a machine tool or of components.

Other assets are commonly valued incorrectly in most firm's financial statements. The value of most firms' plant and equipment is very different from its book value and its replacement value. In many cases, valuable equipment has been fully depreciated or is valued far below its contribution to the firm's revenues. In other cases, machines that cannot be resold are carried at a high value—based upon their acquisition cost, less depreciation.

Management clearly needs at least two different balance sheets. One would be for tax purposes and another would be for its stockholders. It would also be illuminating to prepare a third balance sheet to evaluate the performance of management. The first would be the present conventional balance sheet, while the second would describe management's best estimate of its tangible assets' true value. The third would include management's valuation of the firm's intangible assets and also correct the errors in the conventional measures of tangible asset value.

	Traditional Balance Sheet	Replacement Value	Value to the Company
Plant	$2,000,000	$3,500,000	$4,500,000
Depreciation	1,800,000		
Equipment	$3,000,000	$1,000,000	$6,000,000
Depreciation	200,000		
Total	$3,000,000	$4,500,000	$10,500,000

Figure 15.   Three descriptions of fixed assets for a hypothetical firm

Figure 15 presents three different balance sheets for the same hypothetical firm. This example is enormously simplified, but should nevertheless indicate how much information top management loses if it relies on the information in its traditional balance sheet.

Most executives have absorbed the accounting viewpoint for it is embodied in all financial information they see and rely upon. They are shocked when told that their firm's intangible assets may be far more valuable than their tangible assets. A little reflection leads inescapably to the conclusion that intangibles may be extremely valuable, as the following illustration indicates.

Consider two hypothetical firms with identical plants and equipment, equal numbers of employees, managers, etc. The first produces items that are highly valued by consumers, distributors and retailers because of the firm's imaginative advertising, skilled salesforce and excellent customer service. Its labor force is friendly toward management and ownership and vice versa. Relations among members of top management are extremely cordial and the firm enjoys strong sales support from its excellent distributors. Its suppliers also give it preferential treatment during periods of shortage. For the second firm, none of these conditions is true. The first is highly profitable, while the second is losing money even though its products are equal in quality to those of the first firm. Clearly, the first firm is far more valuable than the second. The reason: The first firm possesses very valuable intangible assets, while the second has many costly intangible liabilities.

Figure 16 lists some of the more common and valuable intangible assets that managements do value but are not included among a firm's assets on its financial statements.

It is difficult enough to place an accurate financial value on many tangible assets. It is far more difficult to assess the worth of intangible assets. Nevertheless, rational management dictates that it be done and with care.

Since intangible assets are often a firm's most precious assets, businesspeople should be very aware of them,

Intangible Assets	Intangible Liabilities
Favorable brand image	Poor brand image
Strong distributors	Weak distributors
Good retailer support	Little retailer support
Good bank connections	Bank not supportive
Easy access to bank loans	No access to bank loans
Excellent credit rating	Poor credit rating
Skilled labor force	Unskilled labor force
High labor morale (low turnover)	Poor labor morale
Close supplier relations	Bad supplier relations

Figure 16.   Common business intangible assets and liabilities

know the many forms they take, and understand their contribution to their firm's success or failure. If they are ignored, businesses will inevitably make some damaging decisions. As was explained in Chapter 3 many businesses value intangible costs either at zero or infinity when they make decisions. Both are manifestly wrong.

The Valuation of Assets

What is the true value to a firm of a particular piece of machinery or any other physical asset that it might purchase? Recognize at the outset that the value of many assets is situational. It often varies from buyer to buyer. It depends upon the circumstances in which the seller finds itself and upon the buyers' and sellers' expectations of future developments. However, in general and simple terms, the value of a machine is the (discounted) dollar value of the extra net income it would produce over its life. If the new machine were to replace an existing present machine, it would be the present value of the stream of extra value (dollar output or sales) it would produce over its life less the added costs associated with its use. More concretely, it would be the added number of units it is expected to produce times the price that the firm receives for this added output less the added cost incurred to acquire and maintain the machine in use. The point to recognize is that assets get their value from what they produce for the organization and not from their resale value. The difference between these two values is often huge.

We therefore conclude that the value of an asset is derived from its expected contributions to the firm's future revenues. This holds true for both tangible and intangible assets and for action proposals. Thus, the value of an executive training program to a firm is the present value of the extra net revenue its executives will produce during their tenure as a result of that program.

Five Steps for Valid Valuations

There are five essential elements or steps in a valid valuation of assets and action programs:

1. Forecast the effects of the assets and projects in question.

2. Be aware of uncertainty and deal with it in a systematic and rational manner.

3. Translate the effects of the firm's actions into monetary terms.

4. Translate future financial returns into their present value to the firm.

5. Decide on an "expected value."

None of these five requirements for accurate valuations of projects is easily met. As a result, valuations of assets and projects almost never are as accurate as they could be. The following discussion of these five steps provides some guidelines for improvement.

1. Forecast the effects of the assets and projects in question

How will the performance of salespersons change if they take a particular training program? How will advertising of a particular content, in specified media and specific dollar amount, affect the behavior of ultimate customers, retailers, distributors and competitors? Experienced executives usually are the firm's best forecasters of the effects of its actions. That is to say, they presumably have the best model of the process to be forecast, even if it remains unexpressed. Statistical forecasting methods rarely can match the intuitive forecasts of senior executives—even though the forecasts of individual executives may vary.

The ability of executives to forecast accurately the outcomes of their actions is limited—not because of their personal shortcomings but because of the great complexity of the phenomena they manage. Unlike the forecasts of physical scientists, the universe of business is highly unstable. Actions that were highly profitable last year may prove disastrous this year because of changes in the business environment, or because it was novel last year but is no longer so. Also, businesses can rarely duplicate exactly in the future the actions they took in the past because of changes in people and in the actions of competitors, among a host of factors. For these and other reasons, executives cannot expect to forecast accurately. The use of computers and elaborate databases does not change that conclusion. However, the development of relevant databases can improve decisions significantly. To be a learning organization, management must distill its experience for application in the future. To do so requires expenditures for recording the major actions taken by the firm and its main competitors and their effects.

There are several qualitative things that executives can do to cope with the limitations of their forecasts. First, they can explicitly identify the various parties that are affected by the project in question. Very often more than one of the following are affected by a firm's actions: labor, distributors, retailers, suppliers, consumers, competitors and government regulators. All too often, executives simply forecast the effect of their actions on costs, profits or sales. Or they limit their forecast to one or two parties that would be affected by their actions

Second, they can and should indicate the chain of effects they expect their actions to produce. For example, when a firm advertises it usually seeks to reach particular targets—certain segments of distributors, retailers and ultimate customers. A rigorous forecast would identify the targets and the percentage of those targets the advertising is expected to reach. In addition, the advertising presumably is intended to influence those targets in a particular way—to change their attitude, to provide information that they will retain, affecting their brand image and brand preference. Not all targets that change their attitude, get information and change their brand image will make a purchase. Consequently, the forecast should estimate explicitly what percentage of target customers who change their image, etc., will make a purchase—and when.

Presumably, executives who recommend that the firm spend large sums on some project have thought through the many effects of that action; that is, they have forecast the chain of effects. This reasoning should be made explicit for an important reason: One can monitor the effects of the firm's actions at the early links in the chain to see whether the program is working. For example, the first link in the chain of effects of an advertising campaign may be to reach particular targets; the second may be to change their attitudes and so on. After the launch of the campaign, the firm should determine whether it is indeed reaching its targets in the expected numbers and changing their opinions in the desired way. If the advertising is not doing so, the campaign should be stopped or modified early rather than late. It is this kind of monitoring of the firm's actions that is the most effective way to cope with the fallibility of their forecasts.

Qualitative Forecasts. Qualitative forecasts offer major advantages over statistical forecasts. But they are not mutually exclusive. Firms should do both. First, qualitative forecasts provide early warning signals if a program is not working. Second, they force the forecaster to identify the potential unintended effects of the firm's actions.

Usually more than one executive in a firm has experience relevant to the valuation of action programs. The final forecast/valuation usually could be arrived at by a consensus of informed executives' opinions. Whether the views of one executive or many, the links in the chain of effects by which the desired result is reached should be made explicit. The actual effects of the action should be matched against the forecast as much as is feasible.

Many executives are impatient with this kind of forecasting. They apparently feel confident that they can estimate the effect on sales of advertising, adding a new salesperson, changing a distributor, etc., on basically an intuitive basis. If pressed, they might be willing to indicate when they expect the sales increase to begin and the rate at which they would rise in the future.

Executives will make better and safer decisions if they take the time to make their forecasts more explicit and detailed. As a minimum, they should identify the parties that might be affected by their action and the chain of effects by which their ultimate objective will be achieved.

Firms can sometimes conduct market tests that reduce the forecasting error of their decisions. The reliability of market test results varies depending upon the thing that is being tested and the methods employed. Where almost no information is available, market tests can be valuable, but they rarely produce accurate predictions.

Mainly, forecasts of the effects of proposed actions are based upon executives' models; that is, their perceptions and interpretations of the firm's recent experience and that of other firms in the same industry and market. Since that is the case, businesses would be wise to record the results of their actions and those of rivals so that they can learn as much as possible from past experience.

Problems in Forecasting. The plain fact is that no one can forecast accurately the results of most business actions. Our understanding of the effects of business actions is limited. One reason is that most are carried out in unique contexts. Another is that their effects are likely to be blurred by other actions taken contemporaneously by the firm and by rivals. Perhaps the main reason forecasts of the effects of business actions are so imprecise is that they vary in content and message. One salesperson is not the equivalent of the others that the firm hired, or a proposed advertising program has different messages that are presented with greater or less skill than recent advertising campaigns. One cannot easily draw conclusions about the effects of business actions from past experience. Still, some executives are better forecasters of the effects of particular kinds of actions than others even if they have equal information and business experience.

Estimates seldom can be supported fully by accurate, relevant information. Even if executives were willing to wait a long time to get the information they desire and to spend very large sums to get it, they would not necessarily get the information they require. That is true if for no other reason than that information available describes the past while decisions affect the future. An information gap is unavoidable.

Executives must simply do the best they can with what they know and can learn. Error is inevitable. They are not responsible for the lack of supporting data. The data does not exist. That does not mean that no factual information would be helpful. To the contrary, executives would be well advised to learn the sources of relevant information and the research techniques that can reduce the likelihood of error.

Considerable research has been conducted on the validity of executives' and others' forecasts. This research has uncovered some very consistent errors. Perhaps the most important and disquieting is that executives and other people tend to stick close to their original positions even when they receive conflicting information.

Computers and sophisticated software make it possible to process mounds of data quickly and cheaply. Consequently, executives can explore many alternative assumptions quickly and at little cost. For major decisions, these advanced methods easily justify their cost. Businesspeople would make their jobs much easier if they fully understood and appreciated the benefits as well as the weaknesses of these methods. At bottom, the validity of the results they produce depends upon the quality of the executives' models and intuitive judgments.

Interestingly, executives generally do not know, even after the fact, what effects certain actions have had and whether the decisions were correct. The effects of any action taken by a firm are affected by other contemporaneous actions it takes, the actions of rivals, changes in the environment and many other things. Occasionally, a poor decision turns out well. Conversely, some carefully made decisions work badly. It is impossible to tease out the precise effects of a particular decision or action on the various parties affected. This is why businesspeople should make an effort to document efforts and thus learn as much as they can from past experience.

2. Be aware of uncertainty and deal with it in a systematic and rational manner

As indicated, executives never know exactly what results their decisions and actions will produce. They rarely can claim that they know exactly what will happen.

The effects of a firm's actions often last a long time. Most business actions produce a stream of effects. The executive must place a monetary value on this stream for that is what an action is intended to produce. To do so, he or she must translate future monetary returns into present values.

The longer the effects of a firm's actions last, the more they are likely to be affected by unexpected developments. Consequently, the decision-maker must estimate the chance that unforseeable developments will enhance or diminish the returns. How can businesspeople foresee the unforeseeable?

Of course, they cannot; however, based on their experience and the record, businesspeople have some impression about the probability that large unexpected events will occur to invalidate their forecasts. As a matter of practice, most businesspeople deal with such uncertainties by adding a contingency factor to their forecasts. Usually, it consists of reducing estimated benefits or increasing expected costs by a substantial percentage— 20 percent is a very commonly used figure. The effect of that practice is to assume that future developments will always be adverse which is unduly pessimistic.

Creating Probability Distribution. One way of accommodating to the difficulty of making accurate estimates is to indicate a range of expected outcomes. Even better, one could list the different outcomes that might occur. Such a list becomes far more valuable if it is combined with an estimate of the likelihood of each outcome; that is, it is stated as a *probability distribution*. Such information presents the executive's view of the possible outcomes of the decision and their likelihood.

Figure 17 indicates a hypothetical probability distribution. Exact probability estimates are not possible but rarely are necessary. Information that indicates even roughly which outcomes are the most and least likely helps to make a rational decision.

Underlying such a probability distribution is an estimate of the effect of some action—purchase of a machine, the addition of sales staff, the conduct of advertising, etc.—

Added Output	Est'd Price	Added Revenue	Probability
6000 units	$75	$450,000	.35
5000	75	375,000	.50
4000	75	300,000	.15

*Figure 17.   Hypothetical probability distribution
of outcomes of a program of action*

plus an estimate of the likelihood of each reasonable outcome. Both elements reflect mainly subjective judgments
that are based upon some information, some experience
and some guesswork.

By putting what one knows and guesses in this
numerical form, one achieves important benefits, but also
creates a risk. The benefit is that a probability distribution
communicates clearly what the decision-maker is forecasting, and this can be compared with the estimates of others.
The risk is that the concreteness of a probability distribution causes some people to give them greater credence
than they deserve.

What is gained by expressing estimated outcomes in
the form of probability distributions? How is it superior to
the alternatives? A common alternative is to have the most
qualified executives express their opinion on the value of
the program. They would be asked whether they believe
the program will produce enough added business to justify
the added cost of $300,000. Or, the question might be
whether they believe that the program would add at least
5,000 units of sales at $75, and will produce over $375,000
of added revenue. Or, they may be asked what are the
chances that this program would produce between 4,000

and 6,000 added units of sales, or add between $300,000 and $450,000 to revenue. None of these responses conveys nearly as much information as the probability distribution.

As every executive knows, it is very difficult to reach an intuitive judgment about how much profit a particular program will produce and to express estimates in the form of a probability distribution. However, unless the outcome of a program is obviously very attractive or very unattractive, developing a probability distribution is decidedly worth doing. It requires decision-makers to make clear the basis for their conclusions. In the act of developing probability distributions, decision-makers are forced to address issues that might be overlooked. It also sharpens their awareness of the things that might happen.

As discussed earlier, monitoring carefully the early effects of actions taken and taking corrective actions quickly is an important way of dealing with uncertainty.

3. Translate the effects of the firm's actions into monetary terms

The direct effects of a firm's actions are rarely financial. They are such things as added sales calls, better trained executives, advertisements read by potential customers, etc. How can executives get from these effects of their actions to monetary results? The answer is another forecast. The executive needs a model that helps to estimate the financial effects of changes in sales calls, advertising impressions, executive training, etc.

The chapter on models described the consequence net model which indicates a hierarchy of effects. The first effects of many business actions are intangible benefits which subsequently become financial rewards. If they do not yield financial benefits in time, they would not contribute to the firm's profitability and would be poor decisions.

4. Translate future financial returns into their present value to the firm

One hundred dollars in hand is worth more than a guaranteed receipt of the same amount two years from now. The difference in value is explained by both the factor of risk (despite a guarantee, you may not receive the money) and by the fact that if you had the money now you could earn something by investing it. The translation of future income into present value only takes account of the second factor. In effect, one takes the rate of return that the firm confidently expects to make upon its investments over the time period of the forecast and *discounts* the returns.

Tables have been prepared that make such adjustments effortless. Figure 18 presents a small section of a table that one would use to translate future income into present values, given one's assumed rate of return. Such adjustments can make a substantial difference in the attractiveness of investments, especially those that yield their returns some years in the future.

It is essential that an adjustment be made for the time at which one receives returns due to the time-value of money. An adjustment is also needed for the risk factor, and no easy device exists that will meet that need.

Present Worth of $1

Year	5%	6%	7%	8%	9%	10%
1	0.9524	0.9434	0.9346	0.9259	0.9174	0.9091
2	0.9070	0.8900	0.8734	0.8573	0.8417	0.8264
3	0.8638	0.8396	0.8163	0.7938	0.7722	0.7513
4	0.8227	0.7921	0.7629	0.7350	0.7084	0.6830
5	0.7835	0.7473	0.7130	0.6806	0.6499	0.6209
6	0.7462	0.7050	0.6663	0.6302	0.5963	0.5645
7	0.7107	0.6651	0.5227	0.5835	0.5470	0.5132
8	0.6768	0.6274	0.5820	0.5403	0.5019	0.4665
9	0.6446	0.5919	0.5439	0.5002	0.4604	0.4241
10	0.6139	0.5584	0.5083	0.4632	0.47224	0.3855
11	0.5847	0.5268	0.4751	0.4289	0.3875	0.3505
12	0.5568	0.4970	0.4440	0.3971	0.3555	0.3186
13	0.5303	0.4688	0.4150	0.3677	0.3262	0.2987
14	0.5051	0.4423	0.3878	0.3405	0.2992	0.2633
15	0.4810	0.4173	0.3624	0.3152	0.2745	0.2394
16	0.4581	0.3936	0.3387	0.2919	0.2519	0.2176
17	0.4363	0.3714	0.3166	0.2703	0.2311	0.1978
18	0.4155	0.3503	0.2959	0.2502	0.2120	0.1799
19	0.3957	0.3305	0.2765	0.2317	0.1945	0.1635
20	0.3769	0.3118	0.2584	0.2145	0.1784	0.1486
21	0.3589	0.2942	0.2415	0.1987	0.1637	0.1351
22	0.3418	0.2775	0.2257	0.1839	0.1502	0.1228
23	0.3256	0.2618	0.2109	0.1703	0.1378	0.1117
24	0.3101	0.2470	0.1971	0.1577	0.1264	0.1015
25	0.2953	0.2330	0.1842	0.1460	0.1160	0.0923
26	0.2812	0.2198	0.1722	0.1352	0.1064	0.0839
27	0.2678	0.2074	0.1609	0.1252	0.0973	0.0763
28	0.2552	0.1956	0.1504	0.1159	0.0895	0.0693
29	0.2429	0.1846	0.1406	0.1073	0.0822	0.0630
30	0.2314	0.1741	0.1314	0.0994	0.0754	0.0573

Figure 18.   Section of a table that translates future returns into present values

5. Decide on an "expected value"

Assume that the forecast of a project's effects has produced a probability distribution like that presented in Figure 18. Is it possible to summarize that information in a single figure that represents an accurate valuation of the underlying project?

Any compression of data causes a loss of information. One can produce a single figure that better describes a large amount of data than any other figure, but it will not inform as well as all the facts. On the other hand, even very intelligent people find it difficult to comprehend and interpret a mass of information. A conclusion about the worth of a project does not flow directly from a mountain of information. How then can one best summarize information about the different outcomes of a project and at what cost in the loss of information? "Expected value" is a single figure that is most commonly used to summarize frequency distributions when frequency distributions are constructed. When large expenditures of funds are involved, executives would be wise to familiarize themselves with the underlying frequency distribution.

To combine estimates of outcomes in many individual years with probabilities of those outcomes in a single number places a burden on a number that it cannot bear. Decision-makers will surely want to examine the expected time-pattern of outcomes. Are they mainly in the near or distant future? Are the most likely outcomes more concentrated among the low or the high levels?

Mainly, executives should examine forecasts to learn if they include a significant "risk of ruin"—an outcome that would be devastating. Such outcomes would not usually be revealed in summary figures like expected value. Ruinous outcomes could be more than offset by extremely high outcomes and concealed in the expected value. A 10 percent chance of a huge profit does not nearly offset a 10 percent chance of a ruinous loss, but the expected value figure treats them as exactly offsetting.

Expected values represent the estimated outcomes weighted by probability figures. For example, the expected value of the probability distribution described in Figure 17 is $390,000, significantly different from the most likely outcome.

Conclusions

Executives who skip any of the steps discussed court error. By taking short-cuts or relying on intuition—sometimes termed "personal practical experience"—decision makers can make serious errors. Granted, the steps required to make careful valuations are demanding and frustrating. They can be quite time-consuming and even may be costly. However, all of these steps are necessary if one is to make a reasonable valuation. If projects and assets are not estimated fairly accurately, a business will do many things not worth their cost and fail to do many things that would be very profitable.

The foregoing pages should explain why valuation of assets and projects is both vital and difficult,and why the difficulties are not confined to intangibles. To place an accurate financial value on physical assets and on propos-als for action basically requires forecasts of the benefits and costs that they produce. It also requires dealing objectively with risk, the present value of future income and methods of compressing mounds of information into manageable form. Little wonder that valuations are perhaps the most daunting tasks of management.

Much of the discussion of valuation revolves around methodological issues—how to forecast the effects of actions that have unstable results. Few actions by businesses can be forecast exactly, yet executives must place a value on them. Often very large financial stakes ride on the validity of those forecasts. How can businesspeople best make those estimates? How can they protect themselves from erroneous forecasts?

The preceding pages have described some of the methods that management scientists recommend to make forecasts. But since few forecasts are "right on the money" and some are badly mistaken, what should management do? First, they should make explicit the conditions they anticipate in the future in concrete terms, indicating what they expect and when. Second, they should monitor developments to see whether they conform to their anticipations, recognizing that they must be prepared for the unexpected. Third, they must be prepared to make changes in their plans and decisions to adapt to unexpected developments. That means they should decide what actions they will take in the event their key assumptions are off the mark. Finally, after the event, they should analyze their forecasts to minimize forecasting errors in the future.

The recommended methods of making forecasts and valuations are complex, require considerable technical skill and can be costly. How should executives adapt to that situation?

First, they should recognize the big difference in the importance of the decisions they make, importance measured by the magnitude of the gain or loss that might result. Second, they should take account of the complexity of the decision for them, which is closely related to the amount of information and experience they have about the subject of the decision. Third, they should consider the cost of additional information and the opportunity cost of their time to collect and interpret it.

At a minimum, executives should be aware of the steps involved in sophisticated decision-making. They should know that their forecasts need to identify the different parties affected by their actions and the chain of effects by which they expect their action to achieve the forecast results. They should know that they need not settle on a single forecast but can, usefully, estimate the likelihood of different outcomes and, even more usefully, indicate the factors that would account for the differences. They should be aware of the meaning of "expected values" and know what they gain and give up to use such data. And, finally, they should be sure to discount future returns to present values and understand what they are assuming when they use such figures.

Because we know these techniques does not mean that they should always be used. To state the obvious, one uses them only when they are worth the effort and cost. With practice and experience, executives usually can determine when it is essential to make decisions with utmost care and when one would be wise to take short-cuts. They will also know that the use of the most sophisticated methods will not guarantee decisions that turn out well. On the other hand, unsophisticated forecasts are subject to many and serious errors.

CONCLUSION

The issues discussed in this book represent the author's view of the most valuable contributions that managerial economists have made that can help executives operating in our highly volatile economy. If mastered, they illuminate complex problems and suggest how best to cope with them.

The business literature of recent decades abounds in new ideas that promise important improvements in business function. Fad has followed fad, some of which have represented significant contributions but most have not. Absent from the business literature in recent decades—at least that part which many executives read—has been some of the most fundamental economic concepts that are relevant to executives' responsibilities. The foregoing chapters include some of the basic concepts one can distill from economic theory that address some of the most basic problems that business executives face.

Some of the chapters, especially those dealing with models and objectives, incorporate some fairly new material. Most of what is contained in this book was discussed and written about by managerial economists since roughly 1950. However, most senior business executives are not familiar with that material and certainly do not understand it well enough to apply it. Managerial economic concepts are not particularly difficult to understand if one approaches them without prior convictions.

However, both so-called common sense and the effect of cost accounting get in the way of understanding for some executives.

The chapters in this book deal only with selected parts of managerial economics. They represent issues where it appears that many executives have not internalized the basic lessons of managerial economics. The material presented represents a rigorous approach to executive decision and action. It calls for explicit rational analysis but does not require mathematical trappings that are repellant to many executives.

Further Reading

Joel Dean, *Managerial Economics*. Prentice Hall: New York, 1951.

Shlomo Maital, *Executive Economics: Ten Essential Tools for Managers*. Free Press: New York, 1994.

Alfred Oxenfeldt, *Cost Benefit Analysis for Executive Decision Making*. American Management Association: New York, 1979.

A. R. Oxenfeldt, D. W. Miller and R. A. Dickinson, *A Basic Approach to Executive Decision Making*. American Management Association: New York, 1978.

Bradley R. Schiller, *The Economy Today*, Fifth Edition. McGraw-Hill: New York, 1991.

ABOUT THE AUTHOR

Dr. Alfred R. Oxenfeldt is Professor Emeritus of Business, Graduate School of Business, Columbia University, where he was a full professor for 29 years. His first position was Statistician in Charge of Surveys for Dun & Bradstreet. Next, he served as Principal Economist in the War Production Board where he remained until he entered the military service during World War II as a Japanese Language Officer.

He joined the faculty of Hofstra University after the War and became chairman of the economics department where he started his long career as an economic consultant to government and business. After he left Hofstra, he became the executive vice president of a consulting firm specializing in economic and management problems.

After six years as a consultant with management responsibilities, he returned to teaching as a full professor of business at the Graduate School of Business, Columbia University.

Pursuant to his academic interests and consulting assignments, he became an international authority in the field of price-setting and anti-trust. He has written extensively in both fields, publishing 18 books and numerous articles. At Columbia, his teaching was mainly in the fields of managerial economics, marketing management, price-setting and competitive analysis.

Dr. Oxenfeldt has authored, among others, the following books: *New Firms and Free Enterprise, Industrial*

Pricing and Market Practices, Economics for the Citizen, Models of Markets, Pricing for Marketing Executives, Marketing Practices in the TV Set Industry, The Marketing Executive in Action, Economic Systems in Action, A Basic Approach to Executive Decision Making, Cost Benefit Analysis for Executive Decision-Making, and *Competitive Analysis.*

Dr. Alfred R. Oxenfeldt, 207 Huntington Drive, Chapel Hill, NC 27514

NOTES

NOTES

NOTES

NOTES

NOTES

NOTES